VOLUME 7

5 SHORT LESSONS TO HELP CHILDREN GROW IN FAITH!

Have you ever wondered: WHAT IS THE MASS?

Did you know that the Mass has been celebrated for a very long time?

We know this because the Eucharist has been part of the Church since the time Jesus instituted it at the Last Supper. The apostles also celebrated it. In fact, around 100 years after the death and resurrection of Jesus, Saint Justin the Martyr wrote:

> On Sunday, Christians get together, and writings of the apostles and prophets are read. The priest then teaches how to put into practice what was read, and prayers are made for the community. Then there is a sign of peace. After that, the bread and wine are brought to the priest, and he gives praise to the Trinity. Afterwards the Eucharist is given to the people.

Does that sound familiar? It should, because he is describing the Mass!

> Now, it's very important to remember that the Mass is not just about a ceremony. The Mass is really all about A PERSON!

Do you know what the Mass is all about?

Take a quiz! The Mass is about:

- **THE CHOIR!**
- **THE FRIENDS YOU SEE THERE!**
- **YOUR PARENTS!**
- **JESUS!**

If you chose Jesus as your answer, you're right! If you chose something else, pay real close attention to the rest of this book!

When you keep in mind that the Mass is all about Jesus, you understand why we do certain things like bowing and kneeling. This is the way we participate. We do it to show respect and love to our Savior.

If a king and queen, or a famous person, came into the room, you would probably show them great respect, right? How much more when we are in the presence of our Savior? That's why in the Mass we sometimes stand, and sometimes kneel, and sometimes sing. We are in the presence of our King!

The Mass is divided into two parts: the Liturgy of the Word and the Liturgy of the Eucharist!

THE WORD "LITURGY" COMES FROM THE GREEK WORD "LEITURGIA," WHICH MEANS "SERVICE OR WORK FOR OTHERS!"

The Mass is God's work, His service. When we come and stay close to Him at Mass, it becomes our work and our service, too! Going to the Mass is special. It is our time with God!

When Mass begins we stand, as the priest, who acts on behalf of Christ, goes to the altar along with his helpers. The color of the priest's robes will depend on the season or feast. The priest then genuflects, kisses the altar, and greets the people with, "The Lord be with you."

At that time, we have the Penitential Act, which is a time when we ask God to forgive our sins.

Next, we sit down to hear the Word of God!

FAITH COMES BY READING THE WORD OF GOD!

We read from the Old Testament, then we pray a Psalm, then we hear something from the apostles, and lastly, we stand to hear the gospel. Why do we stand?  Because the gospel contains the words of Jesus, and standing is a sign of reverence towards Jesus, who is the Word of God!

Then we make the Sign of the Cross on our forehead, lips, and heart! Why do we do that? Because through the reading, God is speaking to you and me, and so we ask God to bless our minds to understand it, our lips so we can share it, and our heart so we can live it!

After that, we sit down to hear what the priest, and in some cases the deacon, have to teach us. They help us to understand God's Word and how to live it! The teaching of the priest or deacon is called a homily!

Next, we recite the Creed. The Creed reminds us of all that we believe. We also pray for the intentions of the Church.

After that, the second part of the Mass begins:

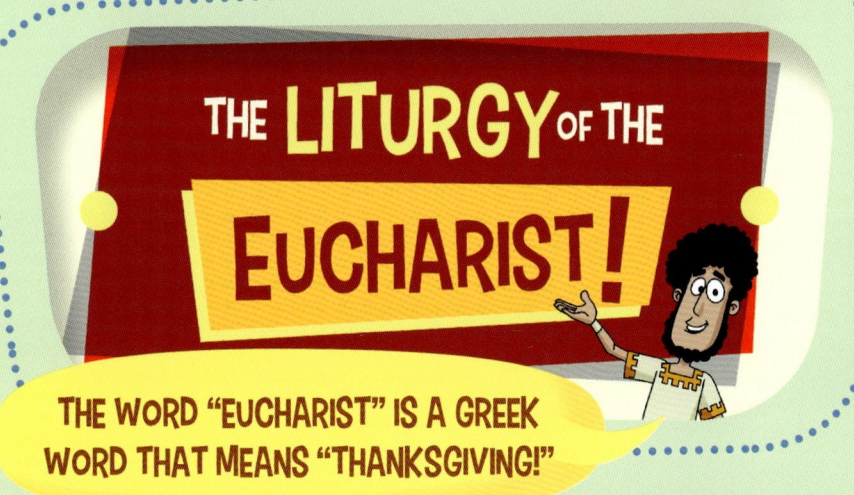

THE WORD "EUCHARIST" IS A GREEK WORD THAT MEANS "THANKSGIVING!"

In this part of the Mass, we show our thankfulness for the birth, death, and resurrection of Jesus! We also take up a collection for the work of the Church, and this is brought to the altar with the gift of the bread and wine!

And we do that because Jesus said:

THIS IS MY BODY WHICH WILL BE GIVEN FOR YOU. THIS IS MY BLOOD WHICH WILL BE POURED OUT FOR YOU. DO THIS IN REMEMBRANCE OF ME.

The priest then prepares the bread and wine. He pours wine into the chalice and then adds some water. This is to show how Jesus is both God and man. He lifts the host of bread above the altar and prays. Then, he does the same with the chalice with wine.

Then as the priest prays over the gifts, we join in praise. People at Mass:

> Holy, holy, holy, Lord God of Hosts, Heaven and Earth are full of Your Glory. Hosanna in the Highest! Blessed is He who comes in the name of the Lord. Hosanna in the Highest!

Then comes the most wonderful, wonderful moment. We all kneel, and after asking the help of the Holy Spirit, the priest uses the words of Jesus over the bread and wine.

> TAKE THIS, ALL OF YOU, AND EAT OF IT, FOR THIS IS MY BODY WHICH WILL BE GIVEN UP FOR YOU. TAKE THIS, ALL OF YOU, AND DRINK FROM IT, FOR THIS IS THE CHALICE OF MY BLOOD, THE BLOOD OF THE NEW AND ETERNAL COVENANT, WHICH WILL BE POURED OUT FOR YOU AND FOR MANY, FOR THE FORGIVENESS OF SINS. DO THIS IN MEMORY OF ME.

The bread and wine are now the body and blood of Christ, our Savior!

We follow by praying the Our Father, then offering each other the sign of peace. We should be at peace with one another when we receive the Eucharist!

After a few more prayers the priest holds up the host and chalice and says:

> BEHOLD THE LAMB OF GOD! BEHOLD HIM WHO TAKES AWAY THE SINS OF THE WORLD. BLESSED ARE THOSE CALLED TO THE SUPPER OF THE LAMB.

PRIEST & PEOPLE:

> LORD, I AM NOT WORTHY THAT YOU SHOULD ENTER UNDER MY ROOF, BUT ONLY SAY THE WORD AND MY SOUL SHALL BE HEALED!

It's at this point that we go to the priest and receive Communion—we receive Jesus! Isn't that wonderful?

Quietly, respectfully, we return to our seats and thank God for His love and forgiveness while the priest cleanses the vessels that were used.

Lastly, we receive a blessing and are told to go in peace! The Mass is over, but our work is just beginning! We walk out the door happy and blessed, ready to be a reflection of God's love to all around us! Isn't that great?

So remember, the Mass is...

- A CELEBRATION OF THE WORD OF GOD.
- A CELEBRATION OF COMMUNION.
- A TIME TO WORSHIP AND THANK GOD.

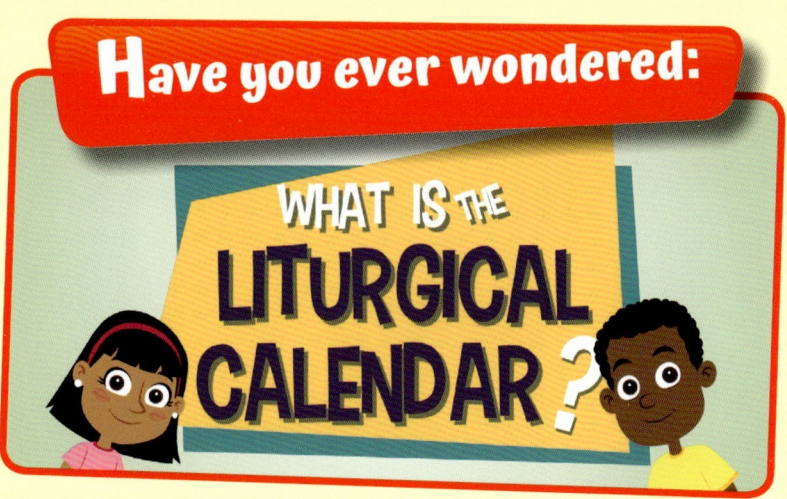

A calendar is a way to keep track of days and weeks, and months and years. By means of a calendar, we are reminded of many things!

A calendar helps to keep our life on track.

Now that you know what a calendar is, do you know what "liturgical" means?

"Liturgical" means "something to do with liturgy." Liturgy describes Christian worship. So, a Liturgical Calendar reminds us of things having to do with our

Christian walk, like holy days of obligation.

A holy day of obligation means there is something we must do. Sunday is a holy day of obligation. It means that we must not miss Mass on Sunday, unless we are very sick.

The Liturgical Calendar reminds us of that.

Other days of obligation, when we must go to Mass, are:

- EASTER
- THE SOLEMNITY OF MARY
- THE ASCENSION OF JESUS
- THE FEAST OF THE ASSUMPTION
- THE SOLEMNITY OF ALL SAINTS
- THE IMMACULATE CONCEPTION OF THE VIRGIN MARY
- CHRISTMAS

These are days we are supposed to go to church. Going to Mass on those days helps us to think about all God has done and continues to do for us. It helps us to remain close and faithful to Him.

Besides the days of obligation, there are also feast days. For example, the Feast day of the Archangels on September 29th.

All these days in the Liturgical Calendar help our faith in God to grow. It reminds us of the way God has worked in the past, and gives us faith in the way God is working now.

Now that you understand the Liturgical Calendar, do you know what the Liturgy of the Hours is? It is the way that some people stop and get close to God hour by hour!

Priests pray the Liturgy of the Hours every day throughout the day, deacons pray it in the morning and evening, and monks and nuns and other people do too! How does it work?

They may wake up very early and begin to pray right away, saying:

LORD, OPEN MY LIPS, AND MY MOUTH WILL PROCLAIM YOUR PRAISE!

They say their prayers, which are based on the Psalms in the Bible, and read about God, and after that they go to their work.

Then at 10:00 in the morning, they stop and pray another set of prayers and do more reading. They do the same thing many times throughout the day. Sometimes, they even get up in the middle of the night to read and pray!

THE LITURGY OF THE HOURS HELPS ME TO STAY CLOSE TO GOD AND TO FOLLOW HIM HOUR BY HOUR.

IT HELPS ME TO KEEP MY PROMISES TO GOD FOR THE SAKE OF HIS KINGDOM!

You don't have to be a monk or a priest or a nun to say the Liturgy of the Hours. There are many people who are not monks or priests or nuns who also pray the Liturgy of the Hours. They may simplify the reading and prayers a little bit, if they are taking care of children or doing their job, but throughout the day, they stop to read and to pray and to make sure they are staying close to God.

There's something else very special about the Liturgical Calendar. It includes a daily reading from the Bible. So, by following it each day, we can read through the Bible many times over! Isn't that great?

THE LITURGICAL CALENDAR

- **HELPS TO KEEP US CLOSE TO GOD ALL THROUGHOUT THE YEAR**

The prayers and Bible reading in the Liturgical Calendar help us to unfold the life of Jesus throughout the year, and to experience Him in the Eucharist! What a great gift the Liturgical Calendar is!

Have you ever wondered:

WHAT IS LENT?

When many people think of Lent, the first thing they think of is having to give up things they like—meat, or chocolate, or movies, or things like that.

Here is a story that might help you understand WHY we give things up during Lent.

Chris and Charlie were going on a vacation with their families. A few days before they left:

MY DOG RAN AWAY!

Although Charlie was very sad, he was hoping the vacation would take his mind off his missing dog.

WE'RE GOING TO HAVE SO MUCH FUN! WE'RE GOING TO GO HIKING, RUNNING, SWIMMING!

Soon they got to his friend's house, but to his dismay!

When they got to their vacation spot, Charlie didn't go exploring or hiking or many of the other things he had wanted to do. He was happy just keeping his friend Chris company.

Why? He was thankful for such a good friend, and for all that his good friend had done for him.

What does this story have to do with Lent? Well, Charlie gave up a lot of things he normally liked to do in order to stay close to his friend, in gratitude for what Chris had done for him.

> **In the same way, during Lent we give up things to keep a close relationship with Jesus.**

The Bible tells us that when Jesus started His ministry, right after He was baptized by John the Baptist, He went into the desert. There He prayed for 40 days, and there He was tempted by the devil to give up the work that He came to do—to save us from our sins.

It was very hard for Jesus to go through that! So why would He do it? Why would He go to all that difficulty, not only in the desert, but later, on the cross?

He did all that for us, because He loved us. And He still loves us today.

So, during Lent, just like Charlie gave up some things to be with his friend Chris, we also give up things that might distract us from our relationship with God.

Lent is a time of REPENTANCE

That's why the church colors change to purple. It's why we start the Lenten season with ashes on our forehead during Ash Wednesday, and we are reminded that like the first man, Adam...

FROM DUST YOU ARE AND TO DUST YOU SHALL RETURN.

During Lent, we remind ourselves that we are God's creation, that He should be the Lord of our life, and that we need to do all we can to keep that relationship sacred and holy and special.

Lent begins on Ash Wednesday and continues to Easter. Lent helps us relive the events of salvation, from Jesus in the desert to His sacrifice on the cross.

It's good to have a time to think about those things, and that's what the season of Lent helps us to do.

In summary:

- LENT IS A SEASON OF REPENTANCE
- A TIME TO GET RIGHT WITH GOD
- AND THAT'S WHY WE GIVE UP THINGS, IN ORDER TO DRAW CLOSER TO GOD!

It's a time to prepare for the season of Easter, when we celebrate Christ's resurrection.

Have you ever wondered: WHAT IS HOLY WEEK AND EASTER?

The Easter season is all about the resurrection of Jesus!

We take time to remember how He rose from the dead, and the events that led to it during Holy Week, when we recount what happened to Jesus according to the Gospels.

One week before His resurrection, Jesus arrived in Jerusalem and was greeted by the people holding palm leaves and shouting:

HOSANNA! HOSANNA! BLESSED IS HE WHO COMES IN THE NAME OF THE LORD!

As wonderful as that was, it was the beginning of Holy Week, one of the most difficult times for our Lord. We recall Jesus' triumphant entry into Jerusalem on Palm Sunday.

On that day, the priest blesses palm leaves. At the end of Palm Sunday, the palms are collected and used as ashes on Ash Wednesday the next year.

After Jesus entered Jerusalem, some of His enemies got jealous and began to look for a way to harm Him.

Four days later, as Jesus and His disciples were getting ready to have supper, He did something they didn't expect.

LORD! WHAT ARE YOU DOING? THAT IS THE WORK OF A SERVANT!

Why did Jesus do that? He would soon go back to the Heavenly Father, so He wanted His disciples to learn an important lesson. By washing their feet, He wanted to show them that they should love and serve each other. Later when they were having supper, He said:

One of you will betray Me.

The disciples were shocked and dismayed! That meant that one of them was going to turn Jesus over to His enemies.

Then Jesus took bread, blessed it and broke it, and gave it to His disciples, saying:

Take and eat. This is My body which is broken for you.

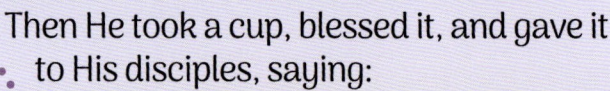

Then He took a cup, blessed it, and gave it to His disciples, saying:

DRINK. THIS IS MY BLOOD WHICH WILL BE POURED OUT FOR THE FORGIVENESS OF SINS.

After supper, Jesus took some of His disciples to pray in the Garden of Gethsemane. He knew He would be killed soon, and His heart was breaking, but Jesus prayed:

FATHER, NOT MY WILL, BUT YOUR WILL BE DONE.

Soon, soldiers showed up. Jesus was arrested and taken away. Just as He had said, Judas Iscariot, one of His disciples, had betrayed Him to His enemies in exchange for thirty pieces of silver. This was a very difficult time for Jesus and

His disciples. Even the Apostle Peter was so afraid that he denied knowing Jesus three times.

We remember this very sad night on Holy Thursday with the Mass of the Lord's Supper.

During the Mass, we remember the example Jesus set for all His followers, teaching us to serve one another. After the homily, the priest will wash the feet of 12 people, or in some cases, the bishop will wash the feet of 12 priests.

Then, after Communion, the consecrated host is carried to the altar of repose and the main altar is stripped of all the ornaments. This represents the time when Jesus was arrested and taken away.

After the Mass, many people remain in adoration throughout the night. It is a good time to think about the sad things that happened to our Lord.

All through the night, Jesus was taken from one important person to another, until His enemies told the governor that Jesus needed to die.

After being hurt with a whip and a crown of thorns, Jesus was made to carry a cross through the city to a place called Golgotha. There He took the punishment for our sins, on the cross.

To remember Jesus' death, we do not celebrate Mass on Holy Friday. Instead we gather to read from the Bible, to think about the cross, and what it cost our Lord to give His life on it for you and me.

Then the Eucharist, which had been consecrated the day before, is given to those present, and everyone leaves, quietly thinking about Jesus and His death.

The Bible tells us that after His death, Jesus was placed in a tomb. That is why the church is empty this night and all throughout the next day, Holy Saturday. This is a good time to think about Jesus' descent to preach to the spirits of the dead.

At some point after His death, Jesus' enemies went to the governor.

BECAUSE JESUS SAID HE WOULD RISE FROM THE DEAD, SEAL THE TOMB AND SET UP GUARDS. THAT WAY HIS DISCIPLES CAN'T STEAL THE BODY AND SAY THAT HE HAS RISEN.

Pilate posted soldiers outside the tomb to keep watch.

And so, on Saturday night, we keep watch by means of the Easter Vigil. When you come to church on this night, you will see a fire outside the church and a large candle. The candle is blessed and lit. The large candle represents Jesus!

As the candle is carried into the church, its light spreads as those present light their candles and pass that same light to others! This represents the Light of Christ spreading to all the world!

After several readings of the Bible, we celebrate Baptism and Confirmation for anyone that is joining the Catholic Church.

At this time we prepare for one of the most exciting events of all history. Why?

JESUS ROSE FROM THE DEAD!

And that is why we celebrate His resurrection on Easter Sunday!

And we continue to celebrate His resurrection for fifty days after! WOW! So don't forget.

Holy Week is a time to remember:

- THE LORD'S LAST WEEK BEFORE HIS DEATH ON THE CROSS.
- HIS EXAMPLE OF SERVICE.
- HIS PROMISE TO BE WITH US IN COMMUNION.
- HIS SUFFERING AND DEATH.
- AND HIS WONDERFUL, POWERFUL, AND AMAZING RESURRECTION!

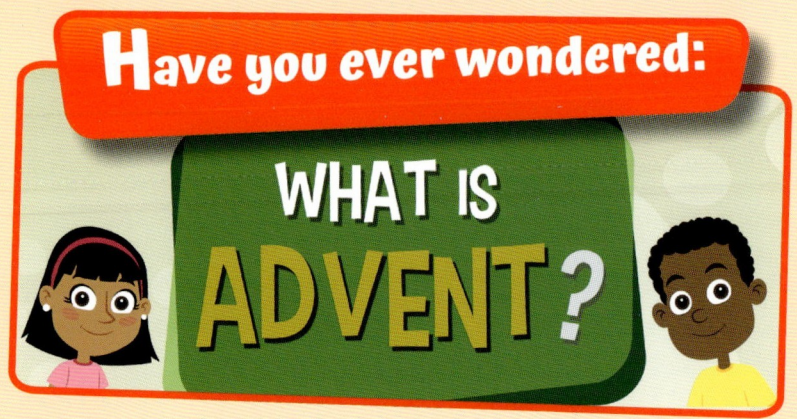

Have you ever wondered: WHAT IS ADVENT?

Right around the end of November everybody starts preparing for Christmas. Decorations go up in stores and people start shopping for presents. But BEFORE Christmas comes another very special time!

ADVENT Advent comes from the Latin word "Adventus," which means "coming!"

It's like when you are expecting a visit from friends and family that you haven't seen in a long time! You think of all the fun times you've had together; you prepare their room and make plans of things to do with them. You look forward to their visit!

It's also like when you're excited about vacation time and you can't wait for it to come!

In the same way that we look forward to things that are special to us, during Advent we look forward to celebrating Christmas!

There are many fun things that happen when we celebrate Christmas:

- PARTIES!
- NO SCHOOL!
- NICE NEW CLOTHES!
- PRESENTS!
- A CHRISTMAS TREE!
- CHRISTMAS CAROLS!

That's good and fun, but it's not really what Christmas is all about.

Christmas is really all about Jesus.

He came to us as a baby 2000 years ago, and someday, He will return just as He promised.

With everything going on around us, it's easy to forget what the real meaning of Christmas is. That's where Advent comes in. Advent helps us to keep in mind WHO Christmas is about and why we stop to celebrate it.

Advent starts with prayer on the Sunday closest to November 30th and ends with evening prayer on Christmas Eve.

One way we observe Advent is with the Advent wreath. Many people use an Advent wreath to help them spiritually prepare for the coming Christmas season. We prepare spiritually by taking time to pray and rid ourselves of anything that displeases God.

You see, Advent is like Lent--a season of repentance. When we repent of the bad things we've done, it always brings us closer to God and brings us greater joy!

The Advent wreath is full of rich meaning! It is usually made up of evergreen branches tied together in a circle. The circle reminds us of what eternal life is like in Jesus, because a circle never ends.

FOR GOD SO LOVED THE WORLD THAT HE GAVE HIS ONLY SON, SO THAT EVERYONE WHO BELIEVES IN HIM MIGHT NOT PERISH BUT MIGHT HAVE ETERNAL LIFE.

You know what that means? It means that if we trust and believe in Him, He will be with us always. This is the good news, that we may have eternal life and live forever with God!

People place four candles on the Advent wreath. Usually three of them are violet and one of them is the color rose!

Each of the four Sundays before Christmas, family and friends gather around the wreath. They'll read something, either from the Bible or another book, that helps them to think about Jesus.

Then, they pray and light a candle in honor of our Lord. As each of the candles is lit, it reminds us of how Jesus brought His light to our world!

On the third Sunday, the rose-colored candle is lit, because by that time, the days to celebrate the birth of Jesus are getting nearer.

Celebrating Advent reminds us of what the season is about, and just like Lent, it helps us prepare and get right with God, so we can celebrate His coming with a clean heart that is full of joy!